Podcast / Show Name:

....

Hosted By ....

Website: ....

email: ....

BOOK FEATURES -

- Weekly Podcast Planner
- Daily Podcast Episode Planner
- Podcast Brainstorming pad
- Podcast Notebook/Journal

PODCAST
PLAN FOR THE WEEK
Month:......... Week No.......

	Guests	Topic/Discussion
Day 1		
Day 2		
Day 3		
Day 4		
Day 5		
Day 6		

DAILY EPISODE PLANNER

Episode Name:.. Date............................

GUEST/OTHER HOST LIST

TOPICS TO DISCUSS

My Personal Preparation

BEFORE SHOW TASKS

➤

➤

➤

➤

➤

➤

AFTER SHOW TASKS

➤

➤

➤

➤

➤

➤

To be published on -

☐ Facebook ☐ Instagram
☐ Twitter ☐ Other-
☐ Patreon ☐ ....
☐ Youtube ☐ ....

Important notes

DAILY EPISODE PLANNER

Episode Name:.. Date..........................

GUEST/OTHER HOST LIST

TOPICS TO DISCUSS

○
○
○
○
○
○
●
○
○
○

My Personal Preparation

BEFORE SHOW TASKS

➤
➤
➤
➤
➤
➤

AFTER SHOW TASKS

➤
➤
➤
➤
➤
➤

To be published on -

☐ Facebook ☐ Instagram
☐ Twitter ☐ Other-
☐ Patreon ☐ ....
☐ Youtube ☐ ....

Important notes

DAILY EPISODE PLANNER

Episode Name:... Date:...................

GUEST/OTHER HOST LIST

TOPICS TO DISCUSS

My Personal Preparation

BEFORE SHOW TASKS

➤

➤

➤

➤

➤

➤

AFTER SHOW TASKS

➤

➤

➤

➤

➤

➤

To be published on -

☐ Facebook ☐ Instagram
☐ Twitter ☐ Other-
☐ Patreon ☐ ....
☐ Youtube ☐ ....

Important notes

DAILY EPISODE PLANNER

Episode Name:.. Date.............................

GUEST/OTHER HOST LIST

TOPICS TO DISCUSS

○
○
○
○
○
○
●
○
○
○

My Personal Preparation

BEFORE SHOW TASKS

AFTER SHOW TASKS

To be published on -

☐ Facebook ☐ Instagram
☐ Twitter ☐ Other-
☐ Patreon ☐ ....
☐ Youtube ☐ ....

Important notes

DAILY EPISODE PLANNER

Episode Name:... Date................................

GUEST/OTHER HOST LIST

TOPICS TO DISCUSS

My Personal Preparation

BEFORE SHOW TASKS

➤
➤
➤
➤
➤
➤

AFTER SHOW TASKS

➤
➤
➤
➤
➤
➤

To be published on -

☐ Facebook ☐ Instagram
☐ Twitter ☐ Other-
☐ Patreon ☐ ....
☐ Youtube ☐ ....

Important notes

DAILY EPISODE PLANNER

Episode Name:... Date.................

GUEST/OTHER HOST LIST

TOPICS TO DISCUSS

My Personal Preparation

BEFORE SHOW TASKS

AFTER SHOW TASKS

To be published on -

☐ Facebook ☐ Instagram
☐ Twitter ☐ Other-
☐ Patreon ☐ ....
☐ Youtube ☐ ....

Important notes

PLAN FOR THE WEEK

Month: Week no:

	Guests	Topics/Discussion
Day 1		
Day 2		
Day 3		
Day 4		
Day 5		
Day 6		

DAILY EPISODE PLANNER

Episode Name:... Date..................

GUEST/OTHER HOST LIST

TOPICS TO DISCUSS

My Personal Preparation

- ○
- ○
- ○
- ○
- ○
- ○
- ●
- ○
- ○
- ○

BEFORE SHOW TASKS

- »
- »
- »
- »
- »
- »

AFTER SHOW TASKS

- »
- »
- »
- »
- »
- »

To be published on -

- ☐ Facebook ☐ Instagram
- ☐ Twitter   ☐ Other-
- ☐ Patreon   ☐ ....
- ☐ Youtube   ☐ ....

Important notes

DAILY EPISODE PLANNER

Episode Name:... Date:..........................

GUEST/OTHER HOST LIST

○
○
○
○
○
○
●
○
○
○

TOPICS TO DISCUSS

My Personal Preparation

BEFORE SHOW TASKS

➤

➤

➤

➤

➤

➤

AFTER SHOW TASKS

➤

➤

➤

➤

➤

➤

To be published on -

☐ Facebook ☐ Instagram
☐ Twitter   ☐ Other-
☐ Patreon   ☐ ....
☐ Youtube   ☐ ....

Important notes

_____
_____
_____
_____
_____

DAILY EPISODE PLANNER

Episode Name: .... *Date* ....

GUEST/OTHER HOST LIST

○
○
○
○
○
○
●
○
○
○

My Personal Preparation

TOPICS TO DISCUSS

BEFORE SHOW TASKS

➤
➤
➤
➤
➤
➤

AFTER SHOW TASKS

➤
➤
➤
➤
➤
➤

To be published on –

☐ Facebook ☐ Instagram
☐ Twitter ☐ Other-
☐ Patreon ☐ ....
☐ Youtube ☐ ....

Important notes

DAILY EPISODE PLANNER

Episode Name:... Date:.........................

GUEST/OTHER HOST LIST

TOPICS TO DISCUSS

My Personal Preparation

BEFORE SHOW TASKS

➤

➤

➤

➤

➤

➤

AFTER SHOW TASKS

➤

➤

➤

➤

➤

➤

To be published on -

☐ Facebook ☐ Instagram
☐ Twitter ☐ Other-
☐ Patreon ☐ ....
☐ Youtube ☐ ....

Important notes

DAILY EPISODE PLANNER

Episode Name:.. Date..........................

GUEST/OTHER HOST LIST

TOPICS TO DISCUSS

My Personal Preparation

BEFORE SHOW TASKS

AFTER SHOW TASKS

To be published on –

- ☐ Facebook ☐ Instagram
- ☐ Twitter ☐ Other-
- ☐ Patreon ☐ ....
- ☐ Youtube ☐ ....

Important notes

Daily episode Planner

Episode Name:.. Date:...................

Guest/Other Host List

Topics to discuss

○
○
○
○
○
○
●
○
○
○

My Personal Preparation

Before show tasks

➤
➤
➤
➤
➤
➤

After show tasks

➤
➤
➤
➤
➤
➤

To be published on -

☐ Facebook ☐ Instagram
☐ Twitter   ☐ Other-
☐ Patreon   ☐ ....
☐ Youtube   ☐ ....

Important notes

_____
_____
_____
_____
_____

PODCAST
PLAN FOR THE WEEK
Month:.......... Week No.......

	Guests	Topic/Discussion
Day 1		
Day 2		
Day 3		
Day 4		
Day 5		
Day 6		

DAILY EPISODE PLANNER

Episode Name:.. Date:............................

GUEST/OTHER HOST LIST

TOPICS TO DISCUSS

My Personal Preparation

BEFORE SHOW TASKS

AFTER SHOW TASKS

To be published on -

- ☐ Facebook ☐ Instagram
- ☐ Twitter ☐ Other-
- ☐ Patreon ☐ ....
- ☐ Youtube ☐ ....

Important notes

DAILY EPISODE PLANNER

Episode Name: .... Date ....

GUEST/OTHER HOST LIST

My Personal Preparation

TOPICS TO DISCUSS

○
○
○
○
○
○
●
○
○
○

BEFORE SHOW TASKS

➤
➤
➤
➤
➤
➤

AFTER SHOW TASKS

➤
➤
➤
➤
➤
➤

To be published on -

☐ Facebook ☐ Instagram
☐ Twitter ☐ Other-
☐ Patreon ☐ ....
☐ Youtube ☐ ....

Important notes

_____
_____
_____
_____
_____

DAILY EPISODE PLANNER

Episode Name:.. Date:..................

GUEST/OTHER HOST LIST

TOPICS TO DISCUSS

My Personal Preparation

BEFORE SHOW TASKS

➤

➤

➤

➤

➤

➤

AFTER SHOW TASKS

➤

➤

➤

➤

➤

➤

To be published on -

☐ Facebook ☐ Instagram
☐ Twitter ☐ Other-
☐ Patreon ☐ ....
☐ Youtube ☐ ....

Important notes

_____

_____

_____

_____

_____

DAILY EPISODE PLANNER

Episode Name:.. Date.................................

GUEST/OTHER HOST LIST

TOPICS TO DISCUSS

My Personal Preparation

BEFORE SHOW TASKS

AFTER SHOW TASKS

To be published on –

- ☐ Facebook ☐ Instagram
- ☐ Twitter ☐ Other-
- ☐ Patreon ☐ ....
- ☐ Youtube ☐ ....

Important notes

DAILY EPISODE PLANNER

Episode Name:.. Date....................

GUEST/OTHER HOST LIST

TOPICS TO DISCUSS

My Personal Preparation

BEFORE SHOW TASKS

➤
➤
➤
➤
➤
➤

AFTER SHOW TASKS

➤
➤
➤
➤
➤
➤

To be published on -

☐ Facebook ☐ Instagram
☐ Twitter ☐ Other-
☐ Patreon ☐ ....
☐ Youtube ☐ ....

Important notes

DAILY EPISODE PLANNER

Episode Name:.. Date..................

GUEST/OTHER HOST LIST

TOPICS TO DISCUSS

My Personal Preparation

BEFORE SHOW TASKS

AFTER SHOW TASKS

To be published on -

- [ ] Facebook [ ] Instagram
- [ ] Twitter [ ] Other-
- [ ] Patreon [ ] ....
- [ ] Youtube [ ] ....

Important notes

PLAN FOR THE WEEK

Month: Week no:

	Guests	Topics/Discussion
Day 1		
Day 2		
Day 3		
Day 4		
Day 5		
Day 6		

DAILY EPISODE PLANNER

Episode Name:.. Date....................

GUEST/OTHER HOST LIST

| |
| |
| |

My Personal Preparation

TOPICS TO DISCUSS

○
○
○
○
○
○
●
○
○
○

BEFORE SHOW TASKS

➤
➤
➤
➤
➤
➤

AFTER SHOW TASKS

➤
➤
➤
➤
➤
➤

To be published on -

☐ Facebook ☐ Instagram
☐ Twitter ☐ Other-
☐ Patreon ☐ ....
☐ Youtube ☐ ....

Important notes

DAILY EPISODE PLANNER

Episode Name... Date...................

GUEST/OTHER HOST LIST

TOPICS TO DISCUSS

My Personal Preparation

BEFORE SHOW TASKS

➤

➤

➤

➤

➤

➤

AFTER SHOW TASKS

➤

➤

➤

➤

➤

➤

To be published on -

☐ Facebook ☐ Instagram
☐ Twitter ☐ Other-
☐ Patreon ☐ ....
☐ Youtube ☐ ....

Important notes

DAILY EPISODE PLANNER

Episode Name:.. Date..................

GUEST/OTHER HOST LIST

TOPICS TO DISCUSS

My Personal Preparation

BEFORE SHOW TASKS

AFTER SHOW TASKS

To be published on -

☐ Facebook ☐ Instagram
☐ Twitter ☐ Other-
☐ Patreon ☐ ....
☐ Youtube ☐ ....

Important notes

DAILY EPISODE PLANNER

Episode Name:.. Date.......................

GUEST/OTHER HOST LIST

TOPICS TO DISCUSS

My Personal Preparation

BEFORE SHOW TASKS

➤

➤

➤

➤

➤

➤

AFTER SHOW TASKS

➤

➤

➤

➤

➤

➤

To be published on -

☐ Facebook ☐ Instagram
☐ Twitter ☐ Other-
☐ Patreon ☐ ....
☐ Youtube ☐ ....

Important notes

DAILY EPISODE PLANNER

Episode Name:... Date...........................

GUEST/OTHER HOST LIST

| |
| |
| |

My Personal Preparation

TOPICS TO DISCUSS

○ ○ ○ ○ ○ ○ ● ○ ○ ○

BEFORE SHOW TASKS

➤
➤
➤
➤
➤
➤

AFTER SHOW TASKS

➤
➤
➤
➤
➤
➤

To be published on -

☐ Facebook ☐ Instagram
☐ Twitter ☐ Other-
☐ Patreon ☐ ....
☐ Youtube ☐ ....

Important notes

_____
_____
_____
_____
_____

DAILY EPISODE PLANNER

Episode Name:... Date:.........................

GUEST/OTHER HOST LIST

TOPICS TO DISCUSS

My Personal Preparation

○ ○ ○ ○ ○ ○ ● ○ ○ ○

BEFORE SHOW TASKS

➤
➤
➤
➤
➤
➤

AFTER SHOW TASKS

➤
➤
➤
➤
➤
➤

To be published on –

☐ Facebook ☐ Instagram
☐ Twitter ☐ Other-
☐ Patreon ☐ ....
☐ Youtube ☐ ....

Important notes

PODCAST

PLAN FOR THE WEEK

Month:.......... Week No.......

	Guests	Topic/Discussion
Day 1		
Day 2		
Day 3		
Day 4		
Day 5		
Day 6		

DAILY EPISODE PLANNER

Episode Name:.. Date:..................

GUEST/OTHER HOST LIST

TOPICS TO DISCUSS

My Personal Preparation

BEFORE SHOW TASKS

AFTER SHOW TASKS

To be published on -

☐ Facebook ☐ Instagram
☐ Twitter ☐ Other-
☐ Patreon ☐ ....
☐ Youtube ☐ ....

Important notes

DAILY EPISODE PLANNER

Episode Name:.. Date.................

GUEST/OTHER HOST LIST

TOPICS TO DISCUSS

○
○
○
○
○
○
●
○
○
○

My Personal Preparation

BEFORE SHOW TASKS

AFTER SHOW TASKS

To be published on -

☐ Facebook ☐ Instagram
☐ Twitter ☐ Other-
☐ Patreon ☐ ....
☐ Youtube ☐ ....

Important notes

DAILY EPISODE PLANNER

Episode Name:.. Date................

GUEST/OTHER HOST LIST

TOPICS TO DISCUSS

○
○
○
○
○
○
●
○
○
○

My Personal Preparation

BEFORE SHOW TASKS

AFTER SHOW TASKS

To be published on -

☐ Facebook ☐ Instagram
☐ Twitter ☐ Other-
☐ Patreon ☐ ....
☐ Youtube ☐ ....

Important notes

DAILY EPISODE PLANNER

Episode Name:... Date:........................

GUEST/OTHER HOST LIST

My Personal Preparation

TOPICS TO DISCUSS

- ◯
- ◯
- ◯
- ◯
- ◯
- ◯
- ●
- ◯
- ◯
- ◯

BEFORE SHOW TASKS

- ➤
- ➤
- ➤
- ➤
- ➤
- ➤

AFTER SHOW TASKS

- ➤
- ➤
- ➤
- ➤
- ➤
- ➤

To be published on -

- ☐ Facebook ☐ Instagram
- ☐ Twitter ☐ Other-
- ☐ Patreon ☐ ....
- ☐ Youtube ☐ ....

Important notes

_____
_____
_____
_____
_____

DAILY EPISODE PLANNER

Episode Name:.. Date:........................

GUEST/OTHER HOST LIST

| |
| |
| |

TOPICS TO DISCUSS

○
○
○
○
○
○
●
○
○
○

My Personal Preparation

BEFORE SHOW TASKS

➤
➤
➤
➤
➤
➤

AFTER SHOW TASKS

➤
➤
➤
➤
➤
➤

To be published on –

☐ Facebook ☐ Instagram
☐ Twitter ☐ Other-
☐ Patreon ☐ ....
☐ Youtube ☐ ....

Important notes

_____
_____
_____
_____
_____

DAILY EPISODE PLANNER

Episode Name:.. Date:........................

GUEST/OTHER HOST LIST

TOPICS TO DISCUSS

○
○
○
○
○
○
●
○
○
○

My Personal Preparation

BEFORE SHOW TASKS

➤
➤
➤
➤
➤
➤

AFTER SHOW TASKS

➤
➤
➤
➤
➤
➤

To be published on -

☐ Facebook ☐ Instagram
☐ Twitter ☐ Other-
☐ Patreon ☐ ....
☐ Youtube ☐ ....

Important notes

_____
_____
_____
_____
_____

PLAN FOR THE WEEK

Month: Week no:

	Guests	Topics/Discussion
Day 1		
Day 2		
Day 3		
Day 4		
Day 5		
Day 6		

DAILY EPISODE PLANNER

Episode Name:... Date...................

GUEST/OTHER HOST LIST

TOPICS TO DISCUSS

My Personal Preparation

BEFORE SHOW TASKS

AFTER SHOW TASKS

To be published on -

☐ Facebook ☐ Instagram
☐ Twitter ☐ Other-
☐ Patreon ☐ ....
☐ Youtube ☐ ....

Important notes

DAILY EPISODE PLANNER

Episode Name: .... Date: ....

GUEST/OTHER HOST LIST

TOPICS TO DISCUSS

○
○
○
○
○
○
●
○
○
○

My Personal Preparation

BEFORE SHOW TASKS

➤
➤
➤
➤
➤
➤

AFTER SHOW TASKS

➤
➤
➤
➤
➤
➤

To be published on -

☐ Facebook ☐ Instagram
☐ Twitter ☐ Other-
☐ Patreon ☐ ....
☐ Youtube ☐ ....

Important notes

DAILY EPISODE PLANNER

Episode Name: .... Date: ....

GUEST/OTHER HOST LIST

○
○
○
○
○
○
●
○
○
○

My Personal Preparation

TOPICS TO DISCUSS

BEFORE SHOW TASKS

➤

➤

➤

➤

➤

➤

AFTER SHOW TASKS

➤

➤

➤

➤

➤

➤

To be published on -

☐ Facebook ☐ Instagram
☐ Twitter ☐ Other-
☐ Patreon ☐ ....
☐ Youtube ☐ ....

Important notes

Daily Episode Planner

Episode Name: .... Date: ....

Guest/Other Host List

My Personal Preparation

Topics to Discuss

○
○
○
○
○
○
●
○
○
○

Before Show Tasks

➤
➤
➤
➤
➤
➤

After Show Tasks

➤
➤
➤
➤
➤
➤

To be published on -

☐ Facebook ☐ Instagram
☐ Twitter   ☐ Other-
☐ Patreon   ☐ ....
☐ Youtube   ☐ ....

Important notes

_____
_____
_____
_____

DAILY EPISODE PLANNER

Episode Name:.. Date:....................

GUEST/OTHER HOST LIST

My Personal Preparation

TOPICS TO DISCUSS

○
○
○
○
○
○
●
○
○
○

BEFORE SHOW TASKS

▶
▶
▶
▶
▶
▶

AFTER SHOW TASKS

▶
▶
▶
▶
▶
▶

To be published on -

☐ Facebook ☐ Instagram
☐ Twitter ☐ Other-
☐ Patreon ☐ ....
☐ Youtube ☐ ....

Important notes

Daily episode Planner

Episode Name:... Date:......................

Guest/Other Host List

TOPICS TO DISCUSS

○
○
○
○
○
○
●
○
○
○

My Personal Preparation

BEFORE SHOW TASKS

➤
➤
➤
➤
➤
➤

AFTER SHOW TASKS

➤
➤
➤
➤
➤
➤

To be published on -

☐ Facebook ☐ Instagram
☐ Twitter ☐ Other-
☐ Patreon ☐ ....
☐ Youtube ☐ ....

Important notes

_____
_____
_____
_____
_____

PODCAST

PLAN FOR THE WEEK

Month:.......... Week No.......

	Guests	Topic/Discussion
Day 1		
Day 2		
Day 3		
Day 4		
Day 5		
Day 6		

DAILY EPISODE PLANNER

Episode Name:... Date:......................

GUEST/OTHER HOST LIST

TOPICS TO DISCUSS

My Personal Preparation

BEFORE SHOW TASKS

➤

➤

➤

➤

➤

➤

AFTER SHOW TASKS

➤

➤

➤

➤

➤

➤

To be published on -

☐ Facebook ☐ Instagram
☐ Twitter ☐ Other-
☐ Patreon ☐ ....
☐ Youtube ☐ ....

Important notes

_____
_____
_____
_____
_____

DAILY EPISODE PLANNER

Episode Name:.. Date:....................

GUEST/OTHER HOST LIST

TOPICS TO DISCUSS

○
○
○
○
○
○
○
●
○
○
○

My Personal Preparation

BEFORE SHOW TASKS

➤
➤
➤
➤
➤
➤

AFTER SHOW TASKS

➤
➤
➤
➤
➤
➤

To be published on -

☐ Facebook ☐ Instagram
☐ Twitter ☐ Other-
☐ Patreon ☐ ....
☐ Youtube ☐ ....

Important notes

DAILY EPISODE PLANNER

Episode Name:.. Date.........................

GUEST/OTHER HOST LIST

TOPICS TO DISCUSS

My Personal Preparation

BEFORE SHOW TASKS

➤

➤

➤

➤

➤

➤

AFTER SHOW TASKS

➤

➤

➤

➤

➤

➤

To be published on -

☐ Facebook ☐ Instagram
☐ Twitter ☐ Other-
☐ Patreon ☐ ....
☐ Youtube ☐ ....

Important notes

_____
_____
_____
_____

DAILY EPISODE PLANNER

Episode Name:... Date:......................

GUEST/OTHER HOST LIST

TOPICS TO DISCUSS

My Personal Preparation

BEFORE SHOW TASKS

AFTER SHOW TASKS

To be published on -

☐ Facebook ☐ Instagram
☐ Twitter ☐ Other-
☐ Patreon ☐ ....
☐ Youtube ☐ ....

Important notes

DAILY EPISODE PLANNER

Episode Name: .... Date ....

GUEST/OTHER HOST LIST

TOPICS TO DISCUSS

My Personal Preparation

BEFORE SHOW TASKS

➤

➤

➤

➤

➤

➤

AFTER SHOW TASKS

➤

➤

➤

➤

➤

➤

To be published on -

☐ Facebook ☐ Instagram
☐ Twitter ☐ Other-
☐ Patreon ☐ ....
☐ Youtube ☐ ....

Important notes

DAILY EPISODE PLANNER

Episode Name:... Date...................

GUEST/OTHER HOST LIST

TOPICS TO DISCUSS

○
○
○
○
○
○
●
○
○
○

My Personal Preparation

BEFORE SHOW TASKS

AFTER SHOW TASKS

To be published on -

☐ Facebook ☐ Instagram
☐ Twitter ☐ Other-
☐ Patreon ☐ ....
☐ Youtube ☐ ....

Important notes

PLAN FOR THE WEEK

Month: Week no:

	Guests	Topics/Discussion
Day 1		
Day 2		
Day 3		
Day 4		
Day 5		
Day 6		

DAILY EPISODE PLANNER

Episode Name: .... Date ....

GUEST/OTHER HOST LIST

○
○
○
○
○
○
●
○
○
○

My Personal Preparation

TOPICS TO DISCUSS

BEFORE SHOW TASKS

➤
➤
➤
➤
➤
➤

AFTER SHOW TASKS

➤
➤
➤
➤
➤
➤

To be published on -

☐ Facebook ☐ Instagram
☐ Twitter   ☐ Other-
☐ Patreon   ☐ ....
☐ Youtube   ☐ ....

Important notes

_____
_____
_____
_____
_____

DAILY EPISODE PLANNER

Episode Name:... Date................................

GUEST/OTHER HOST LIST

TOPICS TO DISCUSS

My Personal Preparation

BEFORE SHOW TASKS

➤

➤

➤

➤

➤

➤

AFTER SHOW TASKS

➤

➤

➤

➤

➤

➤

To be published on -

☐ Facebook ☐ Instagram
☐ Twitter ☐ Other-
☐ Patreon ☐ ....
☐ Youtube ☐ ....

Important notes

_____
_____
_____
_____
_____

DAILY EPISODE PLANNER

Episode Name: .... Date. ....

GUEST/OTHER HOST LIST

TOPICS TO DISCUSS

My Personal Preparation

BEFORE SHOW TASKS

AFTER SHOW TASKS

To be published on -

☐ Facebook ☐ Instagram
☐ Twitter ☐ Other-
☐ Patreon ☐ ....
☐ Youtube ☐ ....

Important notes

DAILY EPISODE PLANNER

Episode Name:.. *Date*......................

GUEST/OTHER HOST LIST

TOPICS TO DISCUSS

○
○
○
○
○
○
●
○
○
○

My Personal Preparation

BEFORE SHOW TASKS

➤
➤
➤
➤
➤
➤

AFTER SHOW TASKS

➤
➤
➤
➤
➤
➤

To be published on -

☐ Facebook ☐ Instagram
☐ Twitter ☐ Other-
☐ Patreon ☐ ....
☐ Youtube ☐ ....

Important notes

_____
_____
_____
_____
_____

DAILY EPISODE PLANNER

Episode Name:.. Date:........................

GUEST/OTHER HOST LIST

| |
| |
| |

My Personal Preparation

TOPICS TO DISCUSS

○
○
○
○
○
○
●
○
○
○

BEFORE SHOW TASKS

➤
➤
➤
➤
➤
➤

AFTER SHOW TASKS

➤
➤
➤
➤
➤
➤

To be published on -

☐ Facebook ☐ Instagram
☐ Twitter ☐ Other-
☐ Patreon ☐ ....
☐ Youtube ☐ ....

Important notes

Daily episode Planner

Episode Name.. Date..................

Guest/Other Host List

Topics to discuss

○
○
○
○
○
○
●
○
○
○

My Personal Preparation

Before show tasks

➤
➤
➤
➤
➤
➤

After show tasks

➤
➤
➤
➤
➤
➤

To be published on -

☐ Facebook ☐ Instagram
☐ Twitter   ☐ Other-
☐ Patreon   ☐ ....
☐ Youtube   ☐ ....

Important notes

PODCAST

PLAN FOR THE WEEK

Month:......... Week No.......

	Guests	Topic/Discussion
Day 1		
Day 2		
Day 3		
Day 4		
Day 5		
Day 6		

DAILY EPISODE PLANNER

Episode Name:... Date................................

GUEST/OTHER HOST LIST

TOPICS TO DISCUSS

My Personal Preparation

BEFORE SHOW TASKS

>
>
>
>
>
>

AFTER SHOW TASKS

>
>
>
>
>
>

To be published on –

☐ Facebook ☐ Instagram
☐ Twitter ☐ Other-
☐ Patreon ☐ ....
☐ Youtube ☐ ....

Important notes

DAILY EPISODE PLANNER

Episode Name:.. Date.........................

GUEST/OTHER HOST LIST

TOPICS TO DISCUSS

My Personal Preparation

BEFORE SHOW TASKS

AFTER SHOW TASKS

To be published on -

☐ Facebook ☐ Instagram
☐ Twitter ☐ Other-
☐ Patreon ☐ ....
☐ Youtube ☐ ....

Important notes

DAILY EPISODE PLANNER

Episode Name:... Date:........................

GUEST/OTHER HOST LIST

TOPICS TO DISCUSS

○
○
○
○
○
○
●
○
○
○

My Personal Preparation

BEFORE SHOW TASKS

➤
➤
➤
➤
➤
➤

AFTER SHOW TASKS

➤
➤
➤
➤
➤
➤

To be published on -

☐ Facebook ☐ Instagram
☐ Twitter ☐ Other-
☐ Patreon ☐ ....
☐ Youtube ☐ ....

Important notes

DAILY EPISODE PLANNER

Episode Name:.. Date:....................

GUEST/OTHER HOST LIST

TOPICS TO DISCUSS

My Personal Preparation

BEFORE SHOW TASKS

AFTER SHOW TASKS

To be published on -

☐ Facebook ☐ Instagram
☐ Twitter ☐ Other-
☐ Patreon ☐ ....
☐ Youtube ☐ ....

Important notes

DAILY EPISODE PLANNER

Episode Name:.. Date..........................

GUEST/OTHER HOST LIST

TOPICS TO DISCUSS

My Personal Preparation

BEFORE SHOW TASKS

AFTER SHOW TASKS

To be published on -

- ☐ Facebook ☐ Instagram
- ☐ Twitter ☐ Other-
- ☐ Patreon ☐ ....
- ☐ Youtube ☐ ....

Important notes

DAILY EPISODE PLANNER

Episode Name:... Date:.........................

GUEST/OTHER HOST LIST

○
○
○
○
○
○
●
○
○
○

My Personal Preparation

TOPICS TO DISCUSS

BEFORE SHOW TASKS

➤
➤
➤
➤
➤
➤

AFTER SHOW TASKS

➤
➤
➤
➤
➤
➤

To be published on -

☐ Facebook ☐ Instagram
☐ Twitter ☐ Other-
☐ Patreon ☐ ....
☐ Youtube ☐ ....

Important notes

_____
_____
_____
_____
_____

PLAN FOR THE WEEK

Month: *Week no:*

	Guests	Topics/Discussion
Day 1		
Day 2		
Day 3		
Day 4		
Day 5		
Day 6		

DAILY EPISODE PLANNER

Episode Name: .... Date: ....

GUEST/OTHER HOST LIST

My Personal Preparation

TOPICS TO DISCUSS

○
○
○
○
○
○
●
○
○
○

BEFORE SHOW TASKS

➤
➤
➤
➤
➤
➤

AFTER SHOW TASKS

➤
➤
➤
➤
➤
➤

To be published on -

☐ Facebook ☐ Instagram
☐ Twitter ☐ Other-
☐ Patreon ☐ ....
☐ Youtube ☐ ....

Important notes

_____
_____
_____
_____
_____

DAILY EPISODE PLANNER

Episode Name:.. Date:..................

GUEST/OTHER HOST LIST

TOPICS TO DISCUSS

○
○
○
○
○
○
●
○
○
○

My Personal Preparation

BEFORE SHOW TASKS

➤
➤
➤
➤
➤
➤

AFTER SHOW TASKS

➤
➤
➤
➤
➤
➤

To be published on -

☐ Facebook ☐ Instagram
☐ Twitter ☐ Other-
☐ Patreon ☐ ....
☐ Youtube ☐ ....

Important notes

_____
_____
_____
_____
_____

DAILY EPISODE PLANNER

Episode Name: .... Date ....

GUEST/OTHER HOST LIST

My Personal Preparation

TOPICS TO DISCUSS

○
○
○
○
○
○
●
○
○
○

BEFORE SHOW TASKS

➤
➤
➤
➤
➤
➤

AFTER SHOW TASKS

➤
➤
➤
➤
➤
➤

To be published on -

☐ Facebook ☐ Instagram
☐ Twitter ☐ Other-
☐ Patreon ☐ ....
☐ Youtube ☐ ....

Important notes

_____
_____
_____
_____
_____

DAILY EPISODE PLANNER

Episode Name:... Date:...........................

GUEST/OTHER HOST LIST

○
○
○
○
○
○
●
○
○
○

My Personal Preparation

TOPICS TO DISCUSS

BEFORE SHOW TASKS

➤
➤
➤
➤
➤
➤

AFTER SHOW TASKS

➤
➤
➤
➤
➤
➤

To be published on -

☐ Facebook ☐ Instagram
☐ Twitter ☐ Other-
☐ Patreon ☐ ....
☐ Youtube ☐ ....

Important notes

_____
_____
_____
_____
_____

DAILY EPISODE PLANNER

Episode Name:.. Date:..........................

GUEST/OTHER HOST LIST

○
○
○

My Personal Preparation

TOPICS TO DISCUSS

○
○
○
○
○
○
●
○
○
○

BEFORE SHOW TASKS

➤
➤
➤
➤
➤
➤

AFTER SHOW TASKS

➤
➤
➤
➤
➤
➤

To be published on -

☐ Facebook ☐ Instagram
☐ Twitter ☐ Other-
☐ Patreon ☐ ....
☐ Youtube ☐ ....

Important notes

DAILY EPISODE PLANNER

Episode Name:... Date:...................

GUEST/OTHER HOST LIST

TOPICS TO DISCUSS

My Personal Preparation

BEFORE SHOW TASKS

➤

➤

➤

➤

➤

➤

AFTER SHOW TASKS

➤

➤

➤

➤

➤

➤

To be published on -

☐ Facebook ☐ Instagram
☐ Twitter ☐ Other-
☐ Patreon ☐ ....
☐ Youtube ☐ ....

Important notes

PODCAST

PLAN FOR THE WEEK

Month:.......... Week No.......

	Guests	Topic/Discussion
Day 1		
Day 2		
Day 3		
Day 4		
Day 5		
Day 6		

Daily episode Planner

Episode Name:... Date.................

Guest/Other Host List

My Personal Preparation

Topics to discuss

○
○
○
○
○
○
●
○
○
○

Before show tasks

▶
▶
▶
▶
▶
▶

After show tasks

▶
▶
▶
▶
▶
▶

To be published on -

☐ Facebook ☐ Instagram
☐ Twitter ☐ Other-
☐ Patreon ☐ ....
☐ Youtube ☐ ....

Important notes

_____
_____
_____
_____
_____

DAILY EPISODE PLANNER

Episode Name:.. Date.......................

GUEST/OTHER HOST LIST

TOPICS TO DISCUSS

My Personal Preparation

BEFORE SHOW TASKS

AFTER SHOW TASKS

To be published on -

☐ Facebook ☐ Instagram
☐ Twitter ☐ Other-
☐ Patreon ☐ ....
☐ Youtube ☐ ....

Important notes

DAILY EPISODE PLANNER

Episode Name:... Date................

GUEST/OTHER HOST LIST

TOPICS TO DISCUSS

○
○
○
○
○
○
●
○
○
○

My Personal Preparation

BEFORE SHOW TASKS

AFTER SHOW TASKS

To be published on -

☐ Facebook ☐ Instagram
☐ Twitter ☐ Other-
☐ Patreon ☐ ....
☐ Youtube ☐ ....

Important notes

DAILY EPISODE PLANNER

Episode Name:.. Date...................

GUEST/OTHER HOST LIST

TOPICS TO DISCUSS

My Personal Preparation

BEFORE SHOW TASKS

AFTER SHOW TASKS

To be published on -

- ☐ Facebook ☐ Instagram
- ☐ Twitter ☐ Other-
- ☐ Patreon ☐ ....
- ☐ Youtube ☐ ....

Important notes

DAILY EPISODE PLANNER

Episode Name:... Date:........................

GUEST/OTHER HOST LIST

TOPICS TO DISCUSS

○
○
○
○
○
○
●
○
○
○

My Personal Preparation

BEFORE SHOW TASKS

❯
❯
❯
❯
❯
❯

AFTER SHOW TASKS

❯
❯
❯
❯
❯
❯

To be published on –

☐ Facebook ☐ Instagram
☐ Twitter   ☐ Other-
☐ Patreon   ☐ ....
☐ Youtube   ☐ ....

Important notes

_____
_____
_____
_____
_____

DAILY EPISODE PLANNER

Episode Name: .... Date ....

GUEST/OTHER HOST LIST

My Personal Preparation

TOPICS TO DISCUSS

○
○
○
○
○
○
●
○
○
○

BEFORE SHOW TASKS

➤
➤
➤
➤
➤
➤

AFTER SHOW TASKS

➤
➤
➤
➤
➤
➤

To be published on –

☐ Facebook ☐ Instagram
☐ Twitter   ☐ Other-
☐ Patreon   ☐ ....
☐ Youtube   ☐ ....

Important notes

_____
_____
_____
_____
_____

PLAN FOR THE WEEK

Month: Week no:

	Guests	Topics/Discussion
Day 1		
Day 2		
Day 3		
Day 4		
Day 5		
Day 6		

DAILY EPISODE PLANNER

Episode Name:.. Date.........................

GUEST/OTHER HOST LIST

○

TOPICS TO DISCUSS

○
○
○
○
○
○
●
○
○
○

My Personal Preparation

BEFORE SHOW TASKS

➤
➤
➤
➤
➤
➤

AFTER SHOW TASKS

➤
➤
➤
➤
➤
➤

To be published on -

☐ Facebook ☐ Instagram
☐ Twitter ☐ Other-
☐ Patreon ☐ ....
☐ Youtube ☐ ....

Important notes

_____
_____
_____
_____
_____

DAILY EPISODE PLANNER

Episode Name.. Date...............

GUEST/OTHER HOST LIST

TOPICS TO DISCUSS

○
○
○
○
○
○
●
○
○
○

My Personal Preparation

BEFORE SHOW TASKS

➤
➤
➤
➤
➤
➤

AFTER SHOW TASKS

➤
➤
➤
➤
➤
➤

To be published on -

☐ Facebook ☐ Instagram
☐ Twitter ☐ Other-
☐ Patreon ☐ ....
☐ Youtube ☐ ....

Important notes

DAILY EPISODE PLANNER

Episode Name: .... Date: ....

GUEST/OTHER HOST LIST

My Personal Preparation

TOPICS TO DISCUSS

○
○
○
○
○
○
●
○
○
○

BEFORE SHOW TASKS

➤
➤
➤
➤
➤
➤

AFTER SHOW TASKS

➤
➤
➤
➤
➤
➤

To be published on -

☐ Facebook ☐ Instagram
☐ Twitter ☐ Other-
☐ Patreon ☐ ....
☐ Youtube ☐ ....

Important notes

DAILY EPISODE PLANNER

Episode Name: .... *Date* ....

GUEST/OTHER HOST LIST

TOPICS TO DISCUSS

My Personal Preparation

BEFORE SHOW TASKS

➤

➤

➤

➤

➤

➤

AFTER SHOW TASKS

➤

➤

➤

➤

➤

➤

To be published on -

☐ Facebook ☐ Instagram
☐ Twitter ☐ Other-
☐ Patreon ☐ ....
☐ Youtube ☐ ....

Important notes

_____
_____
_____
_____
_____

DAILY EPISODE PLANNER

Episode Name:... Date....................

GUEST/OTHER HOST LIST

○
○
○
○

My Personal Preparation

○
○
●
○
○
○

TOPICS TO DISCUSS

BEFORE SHOW TASKS

➤
➤
➤
➤
➤
➤

AFTER SHOW TASKS

➤
➤
➤
➤
➤
➤

To be published on -

☐ Facebook ☐ Instagram
☐ Twitter ☐ Other-
☐ Patreon ☐ ....
☐ Youtube ☐ ....

Important notes

DAILY EPISODE PLANNER

Episode Name:... Date:...................

GUEST/OTHER HOST LIST

TOPICS TO DISCUSS

My Personal Preparation

BEFORE SHOW TASKS

➤

➤

➤

➤

➤

➤

AFTER SHOW TASKS

➤

➤

➤

➤

➤

➤

To be published on -

☐ Facebook ☐ Instagram
☐ Twitter ☐ Other-
☐ Patreon ☐ ....
☐ Youtube ☐ ....

Important notes

PODCAST
PLAN FOR THE WEEK
Month:.......... Week No.......

	Guests	Topic/Discussion
Day 1		
Day 2		
Day 3		
Day 4		
Day 5		
Day 6		

DAILY EPISODE PLANNER

Episode Name: .... Date: ....

GUEST/OTHER HOST LIST

TOPICS TO DISCUSS

My Personal Preparation

BEFORE SHOW TASKS

AFTER SHOW TASKS

To be published on -

- ☐ Facebook ☐ Instagram
- ☐ Twitter ☐ Other-
- ☐ Patreon ☐ ....
- ☐ Youtube ☐ ....

Important notes

_____
_____
_____
_____
_____

DAILY EPISODE PLANNER

Episode Name:.. Date:......................

GUEST/OTHER HOST LIST

TOPICS TO DISCUSS

My Personal Preparation

BEFORE SHOW TASKS

➤

➤

➤

➤

➤

➤

AFTER SHOW TASKS

➤

➤

➤

➤

➤

➤

To be published on -

☐ Facebook ☐ Instagram
☐ Twitter ☐ Other-
☐ Patreon ☐ ....
☐ Youtube ☐ ....

Important notes

_____
_____
_____
_____
_____

DAILY EPISODE PLANNER

Episode Name:.. Date..........................

GUEST/OTHER HOST LIST

TOPICS TO DISCUSS

My Personal Preparation

BEFORE SHOW TASKS

AFTER SHOW TASKS

To be published on -

- ☐ Facebook ☐ Instagram
- ☐ Twitter ☐ Other-
- ☐ Patreon ☐ ....
- ☐ Youtube ☐ ....

Important notes

DAILY EPISODE PLANNER

Episode Name:.. Date..........................

GUEST/OTHER HOST LIST

TOPICS TO DISCUSS

My Personal Preparation

BEFORE SHOW TASKS

AFTER SHOW TASKS

To be published on -

- ☐ Facebook ☐ Instagram
- ☐ Twitter ☐ Other-
- ☐ Patreon ☐ ....
- ☐ Youtube ☐ ....

Important notes

DAILY EPISODE PLANNER

Episode Name:... Date................................

GUEST/OTHER HOST LIST

TOPICS TO DISCUSS

○
○
○
○
○
○
●
○
○
○

My Personal Preparation

BEFORE SHOW TASKS

➤
➤
➤
➤
➤
➤

AFTER SHOW TASKS

➤
➤
➤
➤
➤
➤

To be published on -

☐ Facebook ☐ Instagram
☐ Twitter ☐ Other-
☐ Patreon ☐ ....
☐ Youtube ☐ ....

Important notes

_____
_____
_____
_____
_____

DAILY EPISODE PLANNER

Episode Name:... Date:.......................

GUEST/OTHER HOST LIST

TOPICS TO DISCUSS

My Personal Preparation

BEFORE SHOW TASKS

AFTER SHOW TASKS

To be published on -

☐ Facebook ☐ Instagram
☐ Twitter ☐ Other-
☐ Patreon ☐ ....
☐ Youtube ☐ ....

Important notes

PLAN FOR THE WEEK

Month: Week no:

	Guests	Topics/Discussion
Day 1		
Day 2		
Day 3		
Day 4		
Day 5		
Day 6		

DAILY EPISODE PLANNER

Episode Name:... Date.........................

GUEST/OTHER HOST LIST

My Personal Preparation

TOPICS TO DISCUSS

○
○
○
○
○
○
●
○
○
○

BEFORE SHOW TASKS

»
»
»
»
»
»

AFTER SHOW TASKS

»
»
»
»
»
»

To be published on -

☐ Facebook ☐ Instagram
☐ Twitter ☐ Other-
☐ Patreon ☐ ....
☐ Youtube ☐ ....

Important notes

_____
_____
_____
_____
_____

DAILY EPISODE PLANNER

Episode Name:.. Date................

GUEST/OTHER HOST LIST

TOPICS TO DISCUSS

○
○
○
○
○
○
●
○
○
○

My Personal Preparation

BEFORE SHOW TASKS

➤
➤
➤
➤
➤
➤

AFTER SHOW TASKS

➤
➤
➤
➤
➤
➤

To be published on -

☐ Facebook ☐ Instagram
☐ Twitter ☐ Other-
☐ Patreon ☐ ....
☐ Youtube ☐ ....

Important notes

_____
_____
_____
_____
_____

DAILY EPISODE PLANNER

Episode Name:.. Date:........................

GUEST/OTHER HOST LIST

○
○
○
○
TOPICS TO DISCUSS

○

My Personal Preparation

○
○
●
○
○
○

BEFORE SHOW TASKS

➤
➤
➤
➤
➤
➤

AFTER SHOW TASKS

➤
➤
➤
➤
➤
➤

To be published on -

☐ Facebook ☐ Instagram
☐ Twitter ☐ Other-
☐ Patreon ☐ ....
☐ Youtube ☐ ....

Important notes

_____
_____
_____
_____
_____

DAILY EPISODE PLANNER

Episode Name:... Date..................

GUEST/OTHER HOST LIST

TOPICS TO DISCUSS

My Personal Preparation

BEFORE SHOW TASKS

AFTER SHOW TASKS

To be published on -

☐ Facebook ☐ Instagram
☐ Twitter ☐ Other-
☐ Patreon ☐ ....
☐ Youtube ☐ ....

Important notes

DAILY EPISODE PLANNER

Episode Name:.. Date...................

GUEST/OTHER HOST LIST

TOPICS TO DISCUSS

○
○
○
○
○
○
●
○
○
○

My Personal Preparation

BEFORE SHOW TASKS

AFTER SHOW TASKS

To be published on -

☐ Facebook ☐ Instagram
☐ Twitter ☐ Other-
☐ Patreon ☐ ....
☐ Youtube ☐ ....

Important notes

_____
_____
_____
_____
_____

DAILY EPISODE PLANNER

Episode Name:.. Date:.................

GUEST/OTHER HOST LIST

TOPICS TO DISCUSS

My Personal Preparation

BEFORE SHOW TASKS

AFTER SHOW TASKS

To be published on -

☐ Facebook ☐ Instagram
☐ Twitter ☐ Other-
☐ Patreon ☐ ....
☐ Youtube ☐ ....

Important notes

Made in the USA
Las Vegas, NV
24 November 2023

81428520R00059